Professor Birdsong's
157 DUMBEST THUGS!

Thieves, Thugs & Rogues Series: Book Two

Leonard Birdsong

Winghurst Publications

Professor Birdsong's 157 Dumbest Thugs!
by Leonard Birdsong
© 2020 Leonard Birdsong
All rights reserved. Printed in the USA.

ISBN: 978-0-9979573-5-8 (Kindle)
ISBN: 978-0-9979573-4-1(Paperback)

Winghurst Publications
1969 S. Alafaya Trail / Suite 303
Orlando, FL 32828-8732
www.BirdsongsLaw.com
lbirdsong22@gmail.com

Disclaimer:
The facts that are recounted in the stories in this volume are true and in the public domain, as best as Professor Birdsong can determine from his research of court documents, newspapers, and wire services. The author's commentaries on these stories are his own views and opinions and do not reflect the official policy or position of any Law school, Law firm or other organization with which the author may be affiliated. The opinions provided herein are not intended to malign or defame any religion, ethnic group, club, organization, company, individual or anyone or anything. The author further covenants and represents that the work contains no matter that will incite prejudice, amount to an invasion of privacy, be libelous, obscene or otherwise unlawful or which infringe upon any proprietary interest at common law, trademark, trade secret, patent or copyright. The author is the sole proprietor of the work and all parts thereof.

Permissions:
Cover graphics: ©Khalid S. Birdsong /
http:friedchickenandsushi.com

Book cover design:
Rik Feeney / www.RickFeeney.com

Acknowledgments

I wish to acknowledge Rik Feeney who has been my stalwart book consultant who has made my dreams of being a Humor author come true.

I also wish to acknowledge my son Khalid Birdsong for the cover art he has done for me over the years. He has been paid handsomely.

Professor Birdsong's 157 Dumbest Thugs!

Table of Contents

Acknowledgments   3

Table of Contents   5

Introduction   7

Preface to Book Two   9

CHAPTER 1   11

CHAPTER 2   25

CHAPTER 3   35

CHAPTER 4   41

CHAPTER 5   53

CHAPTER 6   59

CHAPTER 7   65

About the Author   75

Ordering Information   77

Books by
Professor Birdsong   79

Professor Birdsong's 157 Dumbest Thugs!

Introduction

Law Professor Leonard Birdsong lives in Florida where he has taught Criminal Law, Evidence, and Immigration Law. He has written many scholarly legal pieces since joining the legal academy. This is not one of those scholarly pieces!

This trilogy series of Professor Birdsong's newest Dumbest Criminal Stories: Thieves, Thugs & Rogues is written just for fun and enjoyment. It showcases stories from all over the world and contains the kind of many dumb, funny and weird criminal law stories that he has found and written about since 2008. Read them. Laugh at the stories and then go to Amazon.com and choose from his other inexpensive fourteen humor books for more such laughs.

Professor Birdsong's 157 Dumbest Thugs!

Preface to Book Two

157 Dumbest Thugs!

A thug is defined as a violent person, especially a criminal. Thugs are usually thought of as "outlaws," who operate outside of polite society and make their living through criminal means. Historically a thug was a member of a religious cult of robbers and assassins in India. Thugs were devotees of the Hindu goddess Kali. The thugs were known to have a ritual wherein they would waylay and strangle their victims who were usually travelers. The cult was suppressed in the 1830's by the British colonials.

The word thug derives from the Hindi language word "thag" which meant a swindler or bad person. The verb thuggee in India meant the robbery and murder practiced by the thugs according to their rituals.

In America, we often assume that thugs are shady and dangerous people who will do all type of untoward things for their own gain.

This book is about some of the dumbest modern-day thugs you will ever read about. Read on.

Professor Birdsong's 157 Dumbest Thugs!

CHAPTER 1

Thugs from The East Coast

CONNECTICUT: No way to land a job? A woman became so teed off when her job application to Kentucky Fried Chicken was ignored, she hit a manager on the head with a metal pipe. Karielys Ayala, 22 burst into the fast food restaurant in Bridgeport and allegedly took a swing at 45-year-old manager Bhagmattie Persaud – who allegedly fought back by throwing a container of hot water at her face. Both women were charged with assault. Only one woman left with a job.

CONNECTICUT: 120-year prison sentence – she deserves it! In June 2019, a woman who had been convicted of killing her two children in 2015, saying it was God's plan, was sentenced to 120 years in prison without the possibility of parole. LeRoya Moore, now 40, killed her 6-year-old daughter and her 7-year-old son. Her attorneys contend she was in a psychotic state at the time.

CONNECTICUT: The headline reads, "Fiery ER drive-thru." A driver intentionally crashed into a hospital emergency room with a car that burst into flames in February 2018, authorities report. The driver had multiple gas containers in the car when he crashed through an entrance to Middlesex Hospital. Authorities report that the man's motives weren't known. It is further reported that the driver is man in his 20's who is known to Middletown police. A man who lives across the street from the hospital said he heard what sounded like an explosion and saw a man on fire come running out screaming for help. First responders put the man on a gurney and took him to a different hospital.

CONNECTICUT: She Was a real dope! A woman was arrested on Christmas day, 2017, after she allegedly took out a packet of cocaine in plain view and prepared to do a bit of snorting while waiting to be booked on unrelated charges at a police station. Nicole Hunter was charged with possession, interfering with an officer and disorderly conduct in the town of Ledyard.

NEW JERSEY: Kiddie jail mail drug scam. A woman accused of using children's drawings to smuggle drugs to her boyfriend in a New Jersey jail. A K-9 unit at Somerset County jail found Suboxone was concealed in the drawings addressed to inmate Michael Gill officials say. Authorities arrested Gill's girlfriend, Casey Giles 37, on drug smuggling charges.

NEW YORK CITY: The headline read: "No dough for the Booty Grabber." A $2 million lawsuit filed by a Queens's man who was dubbed "Carlos the Booty Grabber" was tossed out by a Brooklyn judge who didn't buy his claims that he was falsely arrested. Alan Radin sued NYC in 2014 after getting handcuffed the year before on charges that he groped two women near St. John's University. Radin, 35, was cleared of forcible-touching and harassment but said that his life had been ruined over the arrests and the moniker he was given in news reports. The Brooklyn judge ruled that the police had probable cause to arrest Radin because he was positively identified by the victims.

NEW YORK: Son of a gun, maybe? The son of Syracuse's police chief was arrested this past summer with six others on drug charges. Chief Frank Fowler's son, Frank Jr., 25, was being held in lieu of $100,000 bail, the local newspaper reported. Fowler and the others were found with drugs in an apartment by officers investigating a noise complaint, police said. Chief Fowler declined to comment on the arrest.

NEW YORK CITY: Lady Godiva she wasn't! We learn that an irate Manhattan judge gave a harsh sentence to an abusive father who forced the mother of his child to walk naked through the winter streets of Harlem for texting other men. The judge lambasted Jason Melo for his views that were derived from outdated medieval interpretation of gender roles that had "belonged to the dark ages." Manhattan Criminal Court Justice sentenced Melo to prison from 2 1/3 years to seven years. Melo had earlier been convicted by a jury on counts of coercion, assault, menacing, aggravated harassment and endangering the welfare of a child.

NEW YORK: Vet Abuse? A man held an 81-year-old marine veteran hostage in a squalid upstate motel room for at least four years in order to steal his benefit checks, authorities report. Perry Coniglio was arrested in July 2016, in his room adjoining the victims at a motel in Highland, New York, 50 miles north of New York City. Coniglio used brute force to get the mentally diminished veteran to cooperate with him. The elderly man has advance dementia. Police say that the vet received a "tremendous amount of money" each month in Social Security benefits, pension checks and food stamps, although investigators would not divulge the exact total. Coniglio is being held in the Orange County Jail in lieu of $15,000 bond.

NEW YORK CITY: The headline read: "Water gun in drag rob." A cross-dressing crook who wore a dress and bra during a Staten island bank robbery admitted he was armed – but with only a water gun. Jordan Wise, 24, allegedly told federal authorities he used the toy to hold up a bank in Stapleton in July while wearing a long black-and-white dress, silver heels, sunglasses, bra and sequined hat, according to the criminal complaint wise turned himself in after police released surveillance video of him allegedly making off with $780 in cash while dressed as a woman. Oh my!

MARYLAND: The headline read, "Prison for bum doctor." A man accused of injecting misbranded silicone into people's rear ends in hotel-room procedures was recently sentenced to 14 years in federal prison after one of his clients died. The prosecution's allocution at sentencing revealed that Vinnie Taylor of Wilmington, North Carolina, pleaded guilty to receiving and selling misbranded silicone for buttock injections that led to a woman's death in March 2014. Taylor, who is not a medical doctor, told clients that the procedure was safe and involved medical-grade silicone.

MASSACHUSETTS: Goldilocks? Police in the town of Framingham say some modern-day goldilocks broke into a family's home – but instead of eating porridge, he helped himself to some wine and passed out. The alleged burglar, Vaugh Buckley, 45, used a brick to break a window of the home where he was found asleep in a child's bed. Yes, an arrest was made.

NEW JERSEY: Pepper spray? It has been reported that a saucy Taco Bell employee left the crew coughing when she released pepper spray after she was fired. Eight workers and two customers got choked up when the woman sprayed the substance in a storage area at a West Long Branch Taco Bell. We learn, further, that no charges were filed against the woman.

NEW JERSEY: Postal Bribery? We learn that two men have admitted bribing postal workers to steal credit cards from the mails. Olagoke Araomi, 22, and Moussa Dagno, 24, both pled guilty to counts of bribery, bank fraud, and aggravated identity theft. They will both be facing up to 47 years in prison when sentenced in September of 2019. Federal Prosecutors said the couple recruited at least six postal service employees to steal credit cards from the mail in exchange for cash bribes, usually $100 per stolen cards.

NEW JERSEY: Sad, sad story – con returns after serving 30 years only to kill his mother. In October 2014, Steven Pratt was ready to begin his life anew. He had served out a thirty-year prison sentence and had gone home to Atlantic City, where his family held a party to welcome him home. Pratt was only 15 when he got into an argument with a next door that he subsequently shot and killed later the same day. Pratt was tried as an adult for murder and began serving his sentence at a maximum-security prison. Thirty years later Pratt was 45 when he got out and returned to the neighborhood where his 64-year-old mother resided. Neighbors maintained that Gwendolyn Pratt was "kind and always impeccably dressed." She took a 6 am bus to work each day. On the Sunday morning after Pratt's release, police found Gwendolyn dead from blunt force injuries to the head. Pratt was charged, and at his initial court appearance, he allegedly wept. No one has guessed that his mother would lose her life less than two full days after her son was granted his freedom. The outcome? Pratt pleaded guilty to manslaughter and was sentenced to 25 years in prison. Could this be the culmination of a juvenile destroyed by adult incarceration???

NEW JERSEY: Up Skirting… In May 2016 Governor Chris Christie signed into law a bill that makes it "up skirting" a crime. The measure criminalizes the surreptitious recording or photographing of a person's undergarments, under the state's invasion of privacy laws. It also makes the act of publishing "upskirt" images an offense, punishable with prison and fine.

NEW JERSEY: Jersey Cop cops to Highway robbery? We learn from a recent report that a member of the Paterson police force has admitted in court to stealing money during illegal traffic stops and then falsifying reports. Authorities report that the officer, 30-year-old, Matthew Torres and others stopped individual and vehicles in Paterson and stole money from the people they stopped. Officer Torres faces up to 30 years in prison after pleading guilty to conspiracy to violate individuals' civil rights. He pleaded guilty in early May 2019.

NEW JERSEY: Jersey "El Docco" opioids arrest. Authorities report that a Jersey doctor who referred to himself as the "El Chapo of Opioids" is facing federal drug charges. Robert Delagente was charged with distributing a dangerous controlled substance and obstruction. Prosecutors provided evidence that Delagente prescribed opioids to patients without seeing them and often allowed them to choose their own dosage. He is also charged with altering medical records to hide his activities. Both charges are punishable by up to 20 years in prison.

NEW YORK CITY: "Batman vs. Gun," read the headline. It appears that a homeless man allegedly pulled a baseball bat on another subway rider just because their bags brushed on the train. Unfortunately, the target of the would-be slugger's rage turned out to be an armed ex-NYPD officer who pulled a revolver to keep the man at bay – then chased him out of a subway station and into the arms of other law enforcement officers.

NEW YORK CITY: Vandal beheads "Diddy." Yes, a vandal caused $300,000 worth of damage when he toppled a statue of Sean "Diddy" Combs at the Madam Tussauds wax museum in Times Square in on February 17, 2019– and beheaded it in the process, police said. The man – whom police describe as in his 20s or 30s walked in the museum and went directly to floor where the waxen look-a-like was displayed. He left the museum before anyone discovered what happened. Mr. "Diddy" Combs did not immediately respond to a request for comment.

NEW YORK: The headline read, "He busted a move and will soon be plain busted by police." A bearded thief awkwardly danced inside an upstate Rotterdam Walmart to distract a clerk while his accomplice made off with $2,000 in cash and electronics, say police who posted a video asking the public for help in identifying the men.

NEW YORK CITY: Vandal beheads "Diddy." Follow up! A week after the above story we learn this information on the "Diddy" beheading. The news: A career criminal turned himself in to police and confessed to toppling the wax statue of rapper "Diddy." Timothy Glover, 44, was charged with criminal mischief in the second degree. A police source described Glover as an "emotionally disturbed person" who is well known to the police. Glover has 24 prior arrests and was takin to a hospital for psychiatric evaluation.

NEW YORK CITY: Round 3: Vandal beheads "Diddy." Follow up! A week after the above follow we find that a Manhattan judge has ordered a psychiatric exam for the career criminal Timothy Glover. We also learn that the judge ruled that Glover be held without bail. We learn, further, that video surveillance showed Glover allegedly spitting on, punching, then stomping and decapitating the wax sculpture. It is still unclear why Glover was angry with the "Diddy" statue.

NEW YORK: There is a lot of nasty symbolism with respect to the evidence in this case – she obviously hated the man. Charlene Mess, 49, of Attica pleaded guilty to manslaughter and faces up to 25 years in prison. Why? The evidence reveals that she hit her farmer husband, Douglas Mess, 52, with a pitchfork, shot him in the head and finally buried him in manure. Mr. Mess had been reported missing by his son, setting off a seven-hour search.

NEW YORK: IDIOT! In the early months of 2019, an upstate woman wanted advice on how to kill her boyfriend. So, she called 911 and asked an operator. Police then went to her home where they found her swinging a leaf-blower attachment at her elderly boyfriend. Zelda Cotton, 54, of Tonawanda, was quickly arrested for bashing the 76-year-old man.

PENNSYLVANIA: On your way to jail you're going! A man stole a wallet in a Judge's chambers in an effort to pay court fees from two previous assault charges he had been slapped with. Steven Rago, 31, was discovered on surveillance camera stuffing a wallet into a pocket of his sweat pants near a payment window at the Allegheny Township District Court. Rago later admitted to stealing the wallet and returned it, police report.

PENNSYLVANIA: "Give her a gift or else," read the headline. A woman sliced her boyfriend with a boxcutter and threatened to kill him because he failed to give her a birthday present, according to police. Georgia Zowacki had been drinking vodka on her 55th birthday when she allegedly slashed her live-in boyfriend David Rea's arm and held the weapon to his throat, police report. Rea took her out for a birthday lunch but didn't buy her a gift, card, or a cake.

PENNSLVANIA: Hair today, gone tomorrow! A jail inmate was arrested for allegedly smuggling 78 doses of LSD, cocaine and meth into jail – in her weave., according to court records. Lashandra Brown, 29, was charged with 18 counts.

PENNSYLVANIA: The headline read; "Swords and stoned." A one-armed man was so mad at his brother-in-law for refusing to allow him to continue to smoke marijuana at his sister's home that he slashed the man's nose with a samurai sword. Todd Clark, 51, first tried to smack his relative with a cane but stumbled and struck his sister instead. Police report that he then grabbed the sword and sliced a two-inch in his brother-in-law's nose. OUCH.

PENNSYLVANIA: Hannibal the cannibal? A man has been ordered to stand trial on charges he threatened a judge by sending her a letter with a picture of Hannibal Lecter – the cannibal played by Anthony Hopkins in "Silence of the Lambs." Gregg Tchirkow, of the town of Monessen, told the court at his preliminary hearing that the cinematic threat against Westmoreland County Judge Meagan Bilik-Defazio was really only a "cry for help." We learn that a motive for the threat may have been because the judge had sent Tchirkow to prison in 2005 on a drug possession conviction.

VERMONT: "Lots of cheddar," read the headline. Police in Burlington are on the hunt for two women who stole nearly $1,000 in cheese. Police have been locked in a cat-and-mouse game with the crooks since they ripped off two stores on April 15, 2019.

VERMONT: What A stink! We learn that a Vermont man recently confessed to spraying liquid manure on a US Customs Border Protection cruiser last summer. Police allege that Mark Johnson, 53, vandalized the cruiser after he went on a rant about why not enough was being done to arrest immigrants in the country illegally.

Professor Birdsong's 157 Dumbest Thugs!

CHAPTER 2

A Line-Up of Florida Thugs

FLORIDA: The headline read, "Cheesed off." A Melbourne man became so enraged when his friend ate his slice of pizza, he whacked him over the head with a golf club. Drew Cywinski, 25, was allegedly high on the synthetic marijuana known as K-2 when he bashed his friend so hard, the golf club snapped in two, the police report revealed.

FLORIDA: The Postman always rings twice. A man who sparked worldwide outrage by killing Pinky, a popular dancing Flamingo at Busch Gardens, was fatally struck by a truck two months before his trial. Joseph Corrao, 48, was killed in early June 2019 near his home in Orlando. Corrao gained notoriety when. During a 2016 visit to the amusement park in Tampa, he violently threw the flamingo to the ground. The flamingo died. He was charged with animal cruelty, jailed for five days and freed while courts debated his competence.

FLORIDA: Wrong food? We learn that an idiot became so mad with his girlfriend when she bought the wrong food for him at, McDonald's, he pelted her with packets of sweet-and-sour sauce, say police. Jesus Ferrer Jr., 30, allegedly flipped out, threw the sauce and then pinned the woman to the floor in a Tampa hotel room. Yes, yes, he was charged with battery.

FLORIDA: It all came out in the end. A jail inmate denied stealing another inmate's cigarettes. However, a strip search by Crestview correctional officers revealed part of blue latex glove protruding from the suspects buttocks. When officers found six Marlboro cigarettes with the filters removed inside the glove, the 18-year-old was charged with theft.

FLORIDA: What a blockhead. It has been reported that a Dunkin' donuts customer attempted to pay for coffee with prescription pain pills, according to police. Richard Bourque, 30, allegedly offered up the pills at a shop in Pinellas Park. When the cashier turned him down, he snatched the coffee and walked out without paying. We learn that the man was later arrested.

FLORIDA: The headline read: "It's a crime of Jurassic proportions." A man wearing a dinosaur costume was arrested after he whipped out a fake rifle and tried to start a flash mob at a public park in the town of Cocoa. Police report that the 19-year-old scared park-goers who thought he was waving a real rifle. Yes, he was arrested for disturbing the peace.

FLORIDA: The headline read: "Caught orange-handed." A Florida inmate was arrested for eating a drawing made with orange crayon – and soaked in liquid speed. Authorities report that Robert Eames, 27, was munching the kiddy art – which featured a smiley-faced sun – when a guard spotted his tasteless snack. It appears that Eanes had several "speed"-drenched pieces of art which had been sent to him in the Broward County jail.

FLORIDA: Police say this lovers' quarrel turned "fowl." A spat between two lovers turned into an assault when Juwan Brown, 23, of St. Petersburg was arrested for allegedly striking his girlfriend in the face by throwing a chunk of fried chicken at her which knocked off her glasses. Police also report that Brown, the fried-food flinger, has a record of domestic violence and maintain that brown also stepped on the woman's foot during the melee.

FLORIDA: Yum Yum sauce? It has been reported that a former Florida restaurant worker was sentenced to seven years in prison for putting deadly plumber's lye into Yum Yum sauce at a Japanese restaurant in the town of Lakeland. Margarito Padilla, 54, acknowledged tainting the sauce because he was unhappy about the working conditions at the eatery. There will be no Yum Yum sauce for his prison meals.

FLORIDA: Freelance stripping. A Florida woman was arrested after she walked into the Baby Dolls gentlemen's club in Clearwater, took off her clothes, got on stage and started dancing for tips. However, the woman, Natalie Behnke, was not employed by the club. It was the real dancers who called the police on her. She was arrested.

FLORIDA: They say this man's 20-minute airport visit was plane nuts. Drew Bronnenburg, 28, after getting into a fight with his girlfriend, is accused of stripping down to his boxers and hopping the fence at Tampa's O. Knight Airport. Once there, he allegedly tried to steal two planes (he did not know how to start them) and drove around in a golf cart and an airport fuel truck before crashing into a building and being charged with burglary, criminal mischief and grand theft.

FLORIDA: A Florida man faces a child-abuse charge after he beat an 8-year-old boy and threatened to feed him to alligators. The child told police authorities that Dereck Dunn, 28, took him to a pond behind their Palm Coast home and made the threat. Of course, Dunn told Sheriff's deputies he was only joking and denied hitting the boy. We learn further that Dunn was able to post a $7,500 bond in order to be released from custody pending trial.

FLORIDA: A face eating psycho…why? The mother of a Florida State University student charged with fatally stabbing a couple and then biting the man's face told police her son had been acting strangely and claimed to have superpowers but had no history of mental illness or of heavy drug use. Mrs. Mina Harrouff called Jupiter police about three hours after her son, Austin Harrouff, 19, stormed out of a restaurant following an argument with his father. She advised police that Austin had been acting strangely for a week and believed he had superpowers and that he contended he was on earth to "protect people." Nevertheless, it was learned later that 45 minutes after he left the restaurant Austin was arrested after being spotted by Martin County police mauling the body and biting the face of John Stevens, 59. Austin allegedly attacked Steven and his wife, Michelle, 53, stabbing them multiple times with a pocketknife while they sat in their garage at their home.

FLORIDA: Young love, dumb love! A teenager allegedly stole his uncle's police uniform and wore it to impress a girl – but he ended up in jail. Isael Lima, 18, of the town of Bellview was charged with impersonating an officer after taking his uncle's uniform and patrol car, and having a friend film him during a traffic stop, according to police.

FLORIDA: Seems she was the biggest demon. We have learned that a self- proclaimed Florida psychic who charged an elderly woman more than $3.5 million for exorcisms and "spiritual cleansing" has pleaded guilty to tax evasion. Sally Johnson, 41, made this money between 2007 and 2014 by promising to rid the wealthy Massachusetts woman of demons.

FLORIDA: OOPPSS – He picked the wrong man! We learn that a man pretending to be a police officer was arrested when he pulled over a plainclothes police detective. Matthew Erris allegedly placed a siren atop his Chevy Trail Blazer and flashed it at the car in front of him, apparently to get the driver to move out of his way near Tampa. Yes, an arrest was made by the detective.

FLORIDA: Silly spat over a hedgehog? A teenager got so mad during a "custody" fight over a hedgehog, she allegedly socked her mother in the face and was arrested. Emma Davisson, 18, of Seminole was packing her things when she tried to take the family pet, police said. When her mother blocked her path, saying the pet belonged to her younger siblings, Davisson allegedly struck her and was charged with battery.

FLORIDA: This dad put a new spin on "Take Your Child to Work Day. It appears that the man allegedly brought his 11-year-old son with him to burglarize a home. Joseph McIntosh, 32, made his son to sit on a St. Petersburg house porch while he ransacked the place, police said. Mr. McIntosh was charged with burglary, child abuse and meth possession.

FLORIDA: "Money can't you brains," read the headline. A woman who had won a $1 million lottery in 2018 was arrested in May 2019, in a heroin case. Karlee Harbsthad, 27, of Port Orange, bought a Gold Rush Doubler scratch-off ticket and had hit the jackpot in May 2018. Despite her new fortune she began working with a ring of opioid and cocaine dealers, officials said.

FLORIDA: She had no sole. A woman got so angry at a police officer for stopping her on the highway, she pulled off her shoes and threw them at his patrol car. Amber Capraro, 31, was walking in the middle of a highway in St. Lucie County when the officer tried to stop her. She allegedly flew into rage and threw her shoes at his car and jumped on the hood. Yes, she was arrested.

FLORIDA: Long distance abuse. A man's parents flew all the way from their home in India to help him beat his wife in Florida, police report. The parents, in their 60's, and their son were all charged with abusing the woman and holding her captive at the man's Riverview home. The wife and her 1-year-old child were moved to a safe place.

FLORIDA: Oh, so weird… It has been reported by police that a naked man broke into an elderly woman's home and played dress-up with her clothes. Joseph Vaglica, 40, of the town of Edgewater, allegedly dashed into the 82-year-old Sylvia Garmond's home through her garage door. Vaglica went straight for her bedroom closet, then waltzed into the kitchen for an unwelcome fashion show. Police were called, and he was arrested on a burglary charge.

FLORIDA: The Business Bandit? It has been reported that the FBI is on the hunt for a dashing Florida crook who robs banks while wearing upscale business attire. The so-called "Business Bandit" sports a GQ-style driving cap, ties and button-down shirts during his stick-ups. He has allegedly pulled off robberies at three Palm Beach County banks.

FLORIDA: Isn't it easier to go to the liquor store? A man was arrested recently for making whiskey in an elaborate moonshine operation. John Ward, 52, allegedly made the bootleg liquor with corn, grinders and gas burners at his property in the town of Milton. State wildlife officers spotted a moonshine still, and officials later found several jugs of the hooch with dates written on them. Ward had paid no liquor tax on his moonshine.

FLORIDA: RATS? A Palm Harbor man who triggered an eight-hour police standoff said later he was just shooting rats in his own yard. Stephen Jonas, 51, was allegedly firing his gun in his home at 3 am on a Sunday morning in November. Police set up a perimeter around the house and tried for hours to contact him. When Jonas finally emerged, he claimed he had simply trying to get rid of the filthy rats, police report.

CHAPTER 3

A Few Thugs of the Old South

ALABAMA: The headline read, "Cap'n Punch." Police report that an Alabama man became so mad when his roommate left a box of Cap'n Crunch cereal open, he beat him up and was promptly sent to jail. Duane Smith, 52, of the town of Moundville, flipped out because he has no teeth and the breakfast food is more difficult to chew when it's stale.

ALABAMA: Praise the Lord and pass the Bible! A jail guard has been charged with trying to smuggle drugs inside a Bible. Kenneth Lawson, 32, of Florence was arrested recently during a shift change when fellow officers found the prescription narcotic Suboxone hidden inside his bible, according to a report by the county sheriff. Lawson was also found with tobacco and was charged with trying to bring contraband into the Lauderdale County jail. Lawson had been working at the jail for only three months at the time of his arrest.

ARKANSAS: "Lucky for these two crooks that Al Capone is dead, read "the headline. The thugs tried to steal a statue of the legendary gangster in a bar that Capone had frequented in Hot Springs, but they accidentally dropped it and broke it. The burglars were arrested and charged with public intoxication. The club owner said it cost him $3,500 for repairs.

GEORGIA: Pure animal cruelty? A man was arrested recently for allegedly force-feeding a goat cocaine and whiskey. Sergio Guzman, a 28-year-old horse trainer, was caught on camera holding the goat's horns while a pal shoved drug in its nostrils at a ranch in Gwinnett County, police said. We learn that the goat was taken to a vet and later adopted.

KENTUCKY: It's best to stay awake on any job, dummy! A man, who broke into a number of cars in the town of Harrodsburg, was arrested sleeping in one of those vehicles, while still wearing a mask and back gloves on his hands. Police authorities report that Matthew Stewart, 35, of Louisville, faces theft, criminal mischief and criminal trespassing charges.

KENTUCKY: Call The fashion police on this guy. It has been reported that a blockhead broke into a funeral home in the city of Leitchfield and snatched a dead man's clothes. The man was caught on surveillance camera peeling off his own clothes before slipping into the dead man's clothes. We learn, further, that he also took the decedent's jewelry and the keys to the funeral home's hearse. No arrest has been made.

KENTUCKY: They Say it was not so smooth a robbery. A thief robbed a gas station in Louisville while armed with a tube of hand lotion, according to police. William Walls, 35, was wearing a mask and carrying a sack in which he indicated he had a gun. Walls snatched a bag of cash – but dropped the sack the sack which contained only hand lotion and no gun. He was soon arrested on charges of armed robbery.

NORTH CAROLINA: Ho, Ho, Ho...Seems times are tough all over. Nicole Mary Scarpone, 26, was arrested for burglary after forcing herself into an apartment—and asking each of the three men inside to give her $10 in exchange for sex. Police reported that Scarpone "indicated that she just showed up to make some quick money.

NORTH CAROLINA: What a dummy! Teon Douglas, 21, believed he had found a safe place to stash his weed -- in some weeds. Teon was outside of the courthouse in the town of Sanford waiting for his hearing on a probation violation when he decided that it would foolish to bring his stash with him into the courthouse. So, he tried to bury it in some bushes outside the courthouse, but police officers spotted what he was doing and arrested him.

SOUTH CAROLINA: What a Doofuss. Franklin Hayes 31 was arrested for meth possession in Newbury South Carolina. On the day of his preliminary hearing Hayes was arrested again at the courthouse with more of the drug on him. When deputies searched him at the entrance to the courthouse, they discovered four grams of meth in his pants pocket.

TENNESSEE: He was "bugged" out. A naked man high on a mixture of bug spray and crystal meth terrorized a family when he broke into their house during dinner and cut his throat in front of them, police said. Danny Hollis, Jr. told police he doesn't remember busting into the Lawrence County house – or sitting naked at their dinner table before slicing his neck and jumping out a second story window.

TENNESSEE: Guilty in church shooting revenge. It has been reported in late-May 2019, a jury in Nashville found a man guilty of first-degree murder in a church shooting two years ago that left a woman dead and seven wounded. Jurors deliberated less than five hours before delivering the verdict against Emmanuel Samson. Samson, 27, is African American; the victims were all white. Samson left a note about a 2015 shooting massacre at a South Carolina black church and aimed to kill to kill at least 10 white churchgoers in revenge, the deputy district attorney said.

TENNESSEE: Calls for help, maybe? Police in Clarksville arrested a woman who kept calling 911 to complain that a man refused to marry her. Hee Orama, 34, made multiple calls to say her beau promised to tie the knot and then chickened out. A week earlier, she kept calling 911 to report she could not find her car. Yes, yes, she was in fact intoxicated, at the time of all the calls.

VIRGINIA: His conduct led to a real "High School!" Shop teacher Dominic Leuzzi, 23, was arrested for allegedly allowing students to smoke marijuana in class at Academy of Virginia Alternative High School in Henrico County. Leuzzi was charged with contributing to the delinquency of minors.

TENNESSEE: They dubbed her the "Kingpin Granny." We learn that Betty Jean Jordan, 75, of the town of Parsons, was arrested in early February of this year after peddling so much morphine and oxycodone police obtained an arrest warrant and found her home in her home that was stuffed with illegal drugs and cash. The search of her home pursuant to her arrest revealed 1,000 prescription pills – mainly opioids – and a wad of $12,000 in her possession. Ms. Jordan who uses a wheelchair didn't go quietly when she was arrested. According to police, officers gave her a break by leaving the premises for some time for her to gather her belongings. When officers returned to take her to jail she had gone on the lam. She was apprehended the next day. Since her arrest prosecutors maintain she had been dealing drugs for 20 years.

VIRGINIA: If at first you don't succeed... A heroin dealer is accused of slipping into an Alexandria hospital to make a sale to a patient who then suffered a second near fatal overdose in two days. Police said Michael Filipowicz, 25, signed into the hospital as a visitor to sell the dope to a 24-year-old man who had been admitted the day before after over-dosing.

CHAPTER 4

Some Mid-West Thugs

ILLINOIS: The headline, He robbed a hot-dog stand then accidently shot himself in the wiener. We learn that a clumsy Chicago bandit gave himself the "shaft" when he tried to stuff his handgun into his pocket and it discharged hitting his genitals. Terrion Pouncy, 19, allegedly barged into the Original Maxwell Street Polish restaurant with a scarf over his face, whipped out a pistol and demanded cash.

ILLINOIS: Three car thefts in 15 minutes, bad driver... Yes, a man stole three cars in 14 minutes on a Saturday in late-June 2019, including two good Samaritans' vehicles. He stole a minivan at gunpoint at 5:25 am, crashed it moments later, stole a Chevy from someone who tried to help him, rolled that car over and then stole a Dodge Avenger from a good Samaritan who tried to aid him – all by 5:57 am. Police caught the 26-year-old thief after a brief chase – in which he crashed again.

ILLINOIS: Who flung poo? Susan Miller of Naperville was so fed up with stepping over dog droppings of her neighbors' dog on her sidewalk she took matters into her own hands. Literally! One day Miller picked up some of the dog droppings (we hope she wore gloves) and flung it at the suspect neighbors' front door. Police charged her with disorderly conduct.

INDIANA: He should have stopped for gas, instead. A man who robbed a BP filling station made off with cash but was caught a short time later. Why? The robber had run out of gas. LaPorte police report that Sean Harris, 33, told the clerk he had a gun and took off with money, food, and cigarettes. No gun was found at his arrest.

INDIANA: Sounds like their own little highway to heaven, doesn't it. Three women enticed three men at the Terre Haute prison into a scheme where they were all charged with sneaking through a hole in the ceiling to have sex with each other. Having found a security camera blind spot, the inmates would climb into the ceiling, drink prison made liquor, play cards, and do the "wild thing."

INDIANA: Who wouldn't be combative after being pulled from a pool of pig poop! Perhaps, there is no need to jail this perpetrator -- this may have been punishment enough. Police hunting a man suspected of running a meth lab found him hiding neck-deep in a pool filled with manure at an Indiana pig farm. After police dragged him out of the feces, he became combative and had to be stun-gunned.

KANSAS: QED! We learn that police in Wichita, had hoped that parking a trailer-mounted radar gun in plain sight along a road notorious for reckless driving would make drivers slow down. Wrong! A few hours after moving the radar gun into place a driver going far beyond the speed limit rammed into the trailer destroying the $3,000 radar gun.

KANSAS: Students, don't try this one in court. This stunt sure blew up in his face! A Kansas defense attorney who wanted to illustrate for jurors the meaning of "imminent threat" pulled out a hand grenade in a Hutchinson court, pulled the pin and put it down on the prosecutor's table. The lawyer said the grenade was a dud. His client was a woman accused of forgery and theft. She claimed a co-defendant had threatened to kill her dog and harm her daughter if she didn't take part in the scheme. The lawyer may face charges.

KANSAS: ERIN GO BRAH! A robbery suspect was arrested in Topeka after she decided to attend the city's St. Patrick Day parade immediately after holding up a convenience store. The 26-year-old woman was spotted by police enjoying the parade after they recognized her from a security video. It was not hard for them to spot her. She was the only person at the parade who wore no article of green clothing.

MISSOURI: Bet that idiot won't try this one again. A thief in Kansas City jumped on the hood of a woman's car armed with a handgun and demanded that she give him the car. The lady did not give him the car! Instead, she drove, with the carjacker on the hood, at a high rate of speed to the nearest police station where she crashed into the building. Yes, the carjacker did receive minor, but not life-threatening injuries just before he was arrested.

MICHIGAN: Doughnuts? A group of dummy car buffs who closed down a freeway to spin doughnuts foiled themselves when they posted a video on social media. Police said footage of a Dodge muscle car doing 360's on the major road led to the arrest of a 25-year-old driver, and six more suspects are being investigated.

MICHIGAN: The headline could've read: "Indecent proposal." I t appears that soon after William Cornelius, 25 popped the question and Sheri Moore, 20, said "yep,' the newly engaged couple went on a shoplifting spree in the town of Bay City. First, we learn that Cornelius swiped a bit of jewelry from Walmart as a gift for his financee. Then the couple went to Spencer's Gifts to allegedly steal a vibrator and a pair of edible panties. Unfortunately, they were caught and spent New Year's Day 2016 in jail.

MICHIGAN: Misfortune? It has been reported that a CEO of a mental health organization in this state allegedly embezzled $500,000 to use on fortune tellers. Ervin Brinker, the former head of Summit Pointe in Battle Creek, admitted spending the money on a palm reader and her husband in Key West, Florida. We understand that Brinker is now facing a 32-month prison stretch in Michigan.

MISSOURI: Oh, Poot! We hear that a criminal suspect brought an undetected weapon to his police interrogation in Kansas City. A detective reported that when asked for his home address, the 24-year-old man "leaned to one side of his chair and released a loud fart.' He continued to be flatulent and the detectives as forced to quickly end the interview. PHEW!

NEBRASKA: They say this this alleged shoplifter couldn't get through the courthouse door without breaking more laws. Joshua Weeks, 25, of the town of Beatrice, kept setting off the metal detector at the gage County courthouse near Omaha when guards allegedly spotted drug paraphernalia on him. Deputies say they found syringes and a spoon that tested positive for meth.

NEBRASKA: Unneigborly? A man was recently sentenced to four years in prison after he was convicted of repeatedly sending strippers to his neighbors' door to dance and get naked. The women would bare their breasts and shout for payment from the family, which included two children. Douglas Goldsberry, 45, of Elkhorn sent them over 75 times since 2013 for his own perverse pleasure.

OHIO: Sexual desperation? A 37-year-old woman charged with having sex with a 13-year-old boy was sent back to jail on a bail violation after she tried to contact the boy by sending him a love note wrapped in a burrito. Prosecutors maintain that the burrito love note was a violation of the no contact provision of Amy Blose's $20,000 bail.

OHIO: Ring, ring, bang, bang... A man tried to answer his cellphone while under nitrous oxide at the dentist's office. Unfortunately, he mistakenly grabbed his pistol and shot himself in the hand. James White, 72, thought he heard his phone ringing and somehow set off his gun – with the bullet going through his hand and grazing his stomach. We learn that the New Carlisle Dental Group is now considering prohibiting weapons. And, none too soon!

OHIO: They were called a pair of tater haters. Two teens robbed a Dayton woman of her groceries – and then proceeded to pelt her with her own potatoes. The woman had been walking home from a grocery store when the teen attacked. She called 911, and the dispatchers asked if they had any weapons. "No, but those potatoes hurt," the woman said.

OHIO: Love makes him do foolish things! They say he was looking for love in all the wrong places, but maybe he just has a rubber fetish. Edwin Charles Tobergta pleaded guilty to public indecency for having sex with a rubber pool float in front of several children. He was sentenced to eleven months in jail. Tobergta of Hamilton had been previously charged with having sex with an inflatable pumpkin and with a pool raft.

OHIO: What an ass.... A 20-year-old man in Ohio was sentenced to three years in prison for tattooing the letter A on the rear end of a 19-month-old baby girl. The baby was not his. The child had been left in the care of Lee Dietrick when the baby's mother went to visit a friend who was in the hospital.

OHIO: Irony at its best maybe... The owner of a gun shop was shot dead in mid-June 2016, when a student attending a firearms-safety class accidently discharged his weapon. James Baker, 64, died at the scene, the KayJay Gun Shop in the town of Amelia. The County Sheriff said that Baker was in a room adjacent to the one where the "concealed-carry class" with 10 students was taking place. One of the participants fired his gun while practicing "weapons-malfunction drills. A neighbor told WCPO-TV in Cincinnati that Baker had spent his life teaching others how to protect themselves. Irony at its best!

OHIO: Greg knows no shame for his deed. A man convicted of trying to steal a TV from Walmart was given the opportunity to choose 30 days in jail or 80 hours standing outside the store wearing a T-shirt reading: "I am a thief." Greg Davenport, 44, of Liberty Township, chose the latter. He said he isn't embarrassed by the punishment. He went on to admit: "I stole, I got punished. That's it."

OHIO: IDIOT! A would-be thief in Cincinnati warned a gas station clerk, "We can do this the easy way or the hard way" – but he apparently did not heed his own advice. Andrew Young, 52, allegedly waved a boxcutter at the Speedway clerk, who immediately knocked him out. We learn Young appeared in court with a black eye and crutches

OKLAHOMA: ZOOM… A man live-streamed his high-speed car chase, and not all of his viewers were pleased. Brandon Hager bragged, "I'm in a high-speed chase, bro!" on Facebook Live as he led police through Oklahoma City, prompting his aunt Ashley Rodriquez to call him and beg him to stop. "I call him just to ask him to see, 'Can you just stop? You're making it worse.'" She said. Police captured Hager after he drove into a pond and attempted to run away from the scene.

WISCONSIN: He stopped a potential crime the hard way? Believing he was about to be robbed, a man pulled out a gun and shot himself. The 20-year-old man was walking in a residential area of Milwaukee at around 12:30 am on a Saturday night in June 2019, when he saw two people approaching and became fearful. He grabbed his gun but shot himself in the process. Police said the wound was not life-threatening.

WISCONSIN: Dad kills son over cake? A Milwaukee father is accused of fatally punching his 5-year-old son because the boy ate some of the cheesecake that the man had gotten for Father's Day. Travis Stackhouse, 29, was charged with first -degree reckless homicide in the child's death in late June 2019. A police complaint indicates that the father told police the son had been injured after falling down the stairs. However, the Medical Examiner's office determined the boy died from blunt force trauma to the abdomen. Police say Stackhouse was angry that his children were eating his cheesecake.

WISCONSIN: IDIOT! Mitchel Pfaff, 25, of La Crosse, was arrested when police saw him attempting to exact revenge on a tree in a park by ripping off a limb. Pfaff explained to the police he was "paying the tree back" because he blamed it for a broken skull he suffered when a friend fell from a branch and landed on him. Idiot!

WISCONSIN: The   headline read, "Look before you light up." It appears that a pothead was recently arrested for firing up his doobie in the worst possible place – the parking space of the local police chief. The pothead and a pal allegedly pulled into a parking lot and started smoking weed without noticing a sign nearby that read, "Glendale Police Department," police report. A city worker noted the strong smell of marijuana coming from the car, and the smokers, ages 20 and 21 were arrested. Ah, youth!

WISCONSIN: Serial toilet clogger… Patrick Beeman, 35, of Sheboygan, was sentenced to 150 days in jail for stuffing plastic bottles in the women's restroom toilets at his work on more than 10 occasions. Beeman, who allegedly damaged toilets at prior jobs, told police he gets urges to do odd things.

WISCONSIN: Taco Bell Shoot out? We learn that when a late-night Taco Bell customer got home and discovered that his order did not include the sour cream he had ordered, he phoned and was told the restaurant had closed for the night but that he could return for a free meal the next morning. That offer did not satisfy the customer's rage, so he returned to the restaurant with a gun, took several potshots at the bulletproof drive-thru window and fled.

WISCONSIN: One can say he jumped at the opportunity. We learn that a drunken driver critically injured himself when he jumped off a 250-foot overpass following a 100-mph police chase. The unidentified 24-year-old made the move of jumping after crashing his 2004 Nissan 350Z on I-94 in Kenosha County.

WISCONSIN: They say this man wasn't going to let getting turned down put a damper on his hot date. John Nolan, 32, of Twin lakes, allegedly torched a diesel storage tank in Antioch, Illinois, and fled home to Wisconsin after a woman rejected him. Yes, he has been charged with arson.

CHAPTER 5

Thugs from Texas and the West

TEXAS: The headline read: "There was a big steak in this chase." A man who stole cuts of beef from a Walmart in east Texas led police on a wild pursuit with speeds topping 100 mph, according to East Mountain police. The police report indicates that along the way, the suspect hurled the stolen sirloins out of the car window before he was caught.

TEXAS: Shoot and run, Uber ride turns deadly. James Booker and another man climbed into the back seat of an Uber car on a Friday in late April 2019. Suddenly Booker's companion "immediately opened fire on him in the back seat, where his companion was," said the Houston Sheriff Ed Gonzalez. Mr. Booker was struck multiple times. The shooter took off on foot after the 2 pm shooting while the Uber driver drove to a nearby intersection and called police. No arrest has yet been made.

TEXAS: "Parenting is really going to pot," read the headline. Border Patrol officers recently pulled over an SUV in Brownsville and found a baby in a car seat – next to 275 pounds of marijuana. Ashley Resendiz 22, and Carla Resendiz, 47, who had hung a "baby on board" sign on the back of their Ford Escape were charged with possession and intent to sell drugs.

TEXAS: Cold cut losses? A woman was arrested for smuggling more than 200 pounds of contraband bologna into the U.S. from Mexico. The driver was travelling toward El Paso when authorities found the sandwich meat stuffed under the floor boards of her car. Police report that the unidentified sausage smuggler was fined $1,000 and her bologna as confiscated by the U.S. Customs Service.

TEXAS: There was no mistake – he wore boxers and not briefs. We learn that a pair of boxer shorts could be the best evidence in solving a robbery. The evidence that is known is that a careless bandito covered his face when he held up a convenience store in Waco, but he accidently flashed his bright blue skivvies during the heist, video footage revealed. Waco police authorities say that people may know the individual and recognize him by his boxer shorts.

TEXAS: He busted out of prison for a home cooked meal! It appears that prison food was so bad that Joshua Hansen, 25, of Dallas, was caught trying to sneak back into a federal prison in Beaumont with a feast – including sausages, chicken, rice and veggies – all in a duffel bag, according to Jefferson County police. Police also say they found that Hansen was hauling a stash of liquor.

TEXAS: There will be no second date! A woman allegedly damaged $300,000 worth of art, including two original Andy Warhol paintings, belonging to a lawyer on a first date. Lindy layman, 29, of Dallas was arrested on charges of criminal mischief for the destruction of Anthony Buzbee's artwork. The police report maintains that the belligerent woman allegedly tore down the pricey paintings from the wall and threw two sculptures.

ARIZONA: His number should be on the no dial list. It has been reported that a minister used his church's telephone number in ads to recruit prostitutes. Walter Brazington, 55, a minister for the All Nations Evangelistic Team tried to lure women to a brothel in the town of Broken Arrow, police report. Preacher Brazington is being accused of buying classified ads seeking "massage therapists."

COLORADO: Where there is a will there is a way… A woman originally thought to have been shocked at the Denver Zoo was just very drunk. The disoriented woman entered the elephant enclosure during the zoo's annual holiday light show and sat down next to electrical wires. No animals were in the enclosure at the time. Zoo officials are still trying to determine how the woman made it past two barriers to get inside the enclosure.

COLORADO: On edge is one thing, getting naked is another! When a woman at the Denver International Airport was told to extinguish her cigarette she freaked out and took off all her clothes, according to a police report. The woman told police she was on edge and had not slept the night before. She was taken to a local hospital. No charges were lodged.

NEW MEXICO: Preteen already has a DWI charge on her record. We learn that a 12-year-old was arrested for stealing her family's car, driving it while inebriated and leading police on a high-speed chase, police said. The 12-year-old and three pals went for a cruise on Highway 54 and were spotted by a patrol officer. They sped off and the car spun out of control hitting a sign. No one was hurt.

NEW MEXICO: Weird weapon? A woman was arrested for assault and battery for hitting her mother with a battery-operated vibrator. Cara Claffy, 35, was recently arrested in Albuquerque after police responded to a call from a woman who claimed she had been attacked. When they arrived at the Claffy home, the suspect's mother, Sheryl Claffy, 60, was bleeding profusely. The mother told police she had been arguing with her daughter when Cara picked up a vibrator and hit her on the head.

NEW MEXICO: Yep, truth in advertising. Police and FBI agents broke into a meth, heroin and cocaine ring allegedly run out of a mechanic shop called "Get Your Fix Automotive" in Pueblo. Undercover agents bought drugs and guns from the shop owner Daniel Vasquez, 30, police allege.

UTAH: Obviously, she loved dogs. A woman who broke into a Man's home claimed it was to pet his dogs. Ryan Spurlock said he was surprised to find the intruder in the kitchen of his North Salt Lake City place at 4 am on a Wednesday morning in June 2019. The woman said she came in when she heard the dogs barking. Spurlock said he wouldn't call the police if the woman left. So, she left.

UTAH: We never learned why she was naked! Sylvia Beagley, 31, stole two cars and led police on a wild chase, all while she was naked. Beagley first stole a car from a man who had been hanging roadside signs advertising his business. Then, as officers chased her, she bailed out of the car leading police to chase her on foot. She then doubled back and jumped into one of the empty police cars and took off before crashing. When caught she was given a blanket and placed under arrest.

CHAPTER 6

Some Thugs from California & the Pacific Coast

CALIFORNIA: The headline read. "Aiding and a-breading." It has been reported that a man was given jail time for a very strange assault in a Safeway grocery store. What kind of assault? It appears that Adam Kowarsh, 39, entered the store and immediately set upon one of the employees and began hitting him with a fresh baguette. The employee did not suffer severe injury and Kowarsh did not explain the reason for his assault.

CALIFORNIA: Buy and bust? A man who chatted up a group he met in a hotel hot tub is now in real hot water Andrew Harris asked the woman and two men what had brought them to the Courtyard by Marriott in Mission Valley, police say. When they joked, they were homeless after their meth lab exploded Harris offered to sell them cocaine and LSD, and the guests, actually narcotics detectives, set up a buy-and- bust. Yes, Harris was busted.

CALIFORNIA: The "high" in this higher power church. We learn that the Citadel Church of la Puente in LA was recently raided for selling marijuana, cannabis waxes, and cannabis edibles. Police report they found $30,000 in marijuana products inside the phony church which has no license to sell weed.

CALIFORNIA: Buy and bust? A man who chatted up a group he met in a hotel hot tub is now in real hot water Andrew Harris asked the woman and two men what had brought them to the Courtyard by Marriott in Mission Valley, police say. When they joked, they were homeless after their meth lab exploded Harris offered to sell them cocaine and LSD, and the guests, actually narcotics detectives, set up a buy-and- bust. Yes, Harris was busted.

CALIFORNIA: Vanity, thy name is man. We learn that a fugitive from the Texas "10 Most Wanted" list was caught because of his boasting in an Instagram post. Christopher Gonzalez, an 18-year-old murder suspect, live-streamed footage of himself showing off a shotgun and other weapons. Dallas police got GPS coordinates off his video and learned he was in Woodland Hill, California. They then alerted local police, who quickly arrested Gonzalez.

CALIFORNIA: Senior citizen drug dealing? Fortuna police recently arrested 79-year-old Barbara Engels on drug charges after receiving a tip that she was allegedly selling meth at her retirement home. Detectives recovered three grams of meth, scales and packaging material at her home at the senior-living facility and arrested her for possession of a controlled substance.

CALIFORNIA: He went straight for the gold… A burglar went straight to the $10,000 worth of Koi goldfish. The thief wearing a brimmed hat and carrying a mesh fishing net, was caught on surveillance video grabbing the giant goldfish from a pond in a Westminister family's back yard. Despite being interrupted by the homeowner, the bandit managed to flee with his catch. Police are seeking the public's help identifying the crook.

OREGON: These jerks needed the fashion police, badly! It appears that spelling-challenged vandals scrawled the message "Satin lives" inside a church. The idiots busted a lock on a message board at the house of worship in Forest Grove – and left behind the would-be ominous message. The probably meant to praise "Satan," not the fabric we call "satin."

OREGON: Munchies, maybe? A lady reportedly went wild after drinking before her Taco Bell run. Diane Wilcox, 39, smashed into garbage cans, nearly hit an elderly couple, and then drove her Mercedes into a ditch en route to the Medford, Taco Bell, police said. We learn further that her blood-alcohol level was 0.55, nearly seven times the legal limit.

OREGON: Terrorism wedding caper. A man became so enraged when he learned he hadn't been invited to a relative's wedding, he falsely reported that his father and brother were planning a terror attack. Sonny Smith, 38, of the town of Clackamas is accused of lashing out at his male kin folk because they received invitation and he didn't.

OREGON: The headline suggested that "A getaway car would be more useful than a getaway tree." It has been reported that a 28-year-old man stole $1,373 from a credit union in Bend and then used some of the money to buy a Christmas tree. When police caught up to him, he was trying to hide behind the tree. Of course, it didn't work. Brett Gillispie said he robbed the credit union because he needed money for rent and Christmas expenses.

OREGON: They snoozed and almost lost. A Portland couple awoke and found a man snoozing on their bedroom floor. They originally believed him when he told them he only needed some sleep. However, after they got him out of their house, the couple realized he had stolen their wallets, cellphones and a tablet computer, police report. Authorities credit a GPS App on the stolen phones, which led them straight to the suspect Ervin Solomon, 64, who was hiding under a nearby porch

CALIFORNIA: The headline read, "Give us a brake." Authorities in Orange County report that 1,000 bicycles – many of them stolen – were discovered in a secret bunker below a homeless encampment. Officials were clearing away trash when they spied a trap door leading to the bike stash near the Santa Ana River in the county.

CALIFORNIA: Finders' keepers, losers' weepers? In El Cerrito on a September day police found a man on the street trying to break security tags off 152 bottles of Jack Daniels whiskey. The 20-year-old told police that he had just happened to have found all the bottles of bourbon, worth about $4,400. Police did not make an immediate arrest but took the man's name and address and confiscated the liquor. Police theorize that the whiskey was probably stolen from nearby supermarkets.

WASHINGTON: Police and prosecutors are awaiting Satan to take the witness stand in his own defense. A woman accused of stealing $73,000 from the Arlington church where she worked said the devil told her to do it. "Satan had a big part in the theft," the woman said. They always make Satan the scapegoat!

WASHINGTON: A Rocky Balboa prenuptial party! A woman was arrested for allegedly beating up her fiancé at their prenuptial party when her son caught him making out with one of her friends. Police say the woman tackled and punched him and broke his glasses. There was no word on whether the wedding was still on.

WASHINGTON: This is a shocking story. A lady whose husband was leaving her got back at him by allegedly rewiring his power tools to deliver a powerful electric shock when he used them. She was arrested after he was knocked to the ground while using a 220-volt table saw.

CHAPTER 7

Thugs from Abroad

AUSTRIA: They were not jet fumes! A commercial flight had to make an emergency landing in Austria when a fight broke out over a man who reportedly wouldn't stop loudly passing gas. The Transavia Airlines flight was in route from Dubai to Amsterdam when two fellow fliers asked the stinker to control himself. When he refused, angry words and then punches were exchanged. Amid the mayhem the flight alit in Austria.

AUSTRIA: Burqa Ban? A man in a shark costume was given a fine for covering his face. The worker was dressed as a mascot outside the McShark Computer shop in Vienna, when he was asked by police to remove the shark head. He refused, explaining "I'm just doing my job," according to a report, and was fined $176. It appears that Austria has a strict ban against burqa wearing and anyone else who covers their entire face in public.

CANADA: Talk about irony – this is it. We learn that two women broke out of jail only to be caught a day later. Kelsie Mast, 23, and Samantha Toope, 20, jumped the fence at the Edmonton Institution for Women on a Monday night. The fugitives were arrested the next day at SideQuests Adventures, an adventure park "escape room," where people pay to solve puzzles that will unlock the doors of mock dungeons.

CANADA: The jailhouse wallet is used once again. An Ottawa man was sentenced recently to two years in prison for breaking into a jail with a "buttload" of illegal drugs. Damian O'Reilly, 20, was apprehended for smuggling marijuana, matches, tobacco and rolling papers into the Ottawa Wa-Carleton Detention Center last year. Jail authorities discovered that O'Reilly was hiding the contraband inside eight Kinder Surprise chocolate eggs stuffed in his rectum.

CANADA: A real high-tech Hamburglar. A fraudster recently hacked into a customer's McDonald App and blew thousands of dollars on fast food. The crook ordered more than $2,000 in McFlurries, Big Macs, Chicken McNuggets and other food at several Golden Arches locations in Montreal.

CHINA: Dancing on the ceiling? A man is facing six months in jail after he climbed on top of his car – while it was still moving. The man was caught on camera standing on the white car's roof and waving his arms around as he drove through Bengou City. At one point, it appears the man could be seen sitting in the sun roof and steering with his feet. When he saw traffic police he jumped back into the driver's seat and tried to flee but was caught when he drove onto a dead-end street.

DENMARK: They report he got a ride to central booking. A drug dealer's freedom ended quickly after he jumped in a police car, thinking it was a taxi. It is reported that the police were happy to see him, since he was carrying around 1,000 joints. Copenhagen police tweeted about the arrest to the public after arresting the unnamed man.

EGYPT: Shot in the gonads? A groom-to-be's last night as a bachelor ended with a bang – when he was accidently shot in the genitals. Osman Al-A, 29, was out partying with his buds when one friend fired off the celebratory gunshots. The victim was left serious wounded with injures to his penis, thigh and hand, authorities report. It was not immediately known if he made it to his wedding.

GERMANY: She needed a bigger allowance. In a bid to get ransom money from her father, we learn a 13-year-old girl staged her own kidnapping. The unidentified Berlin teen teamed up with an 18-year-old pal who demanded two payments of $4,500. Almost 300 police officers with dogs scoured the city, only to learn she was fine.

GERMANY: Keeping trouble from brewing? It has been reported that German police confiscated 1,000 gallons of beer from a group of neo-Nazis organizing a festival. The beer ban happened after a court banned beer from the event to reduce the chance of violence.

INDIA: OUCH! A woman became so enraged at her lover for planning to marry someone else that she cut off his penis. The 26-year-old man, known as Irshad met up with his girlfriend one last time in the town of Kattipuram. However, when she learned he had agreed to an arranged marriage with another woman she flew into a fit of rage and chopped off his member with a knife. There is no information about her arrest. And we do not know whether the penis was surgically reattached.

IRELAND: The headline read, "He hit the bottle, a ditch, and himself." Police said they found Brian Fogg, 27, behind the wheel of a car stuck in a ditch in Belfast. However, when they asked him to take a blood-alcohol test, he hit himself in the face three times, causing himself to bleed so police would have to give him first aid. Nevertheless, Mr. Fogg was charged with criminal mischief and operating a motor vehicle while under the influence.

KENYA: Keystone cops in search of a TV set. In May of 2019 police in western Kenya deserted their station house to go search for a TV set to watch a soccer match. The good news is they found one in at a shopping mall. The bad news is thieves sneaked into the station house while they were away and stole three guns and ammunition.

MEXICO: Dangerous spy hole! A man in the town of Peurto Penasco had to be rescued after accidently trapping himself in a hole he dug to spy on his former girlfriend. The Sonora state attorney general's office said the man, 50, spent days digging the hole under his former girlfriend's home. We learn that the man had been court ordered to stay away from the girlfriend and is now in jail, but alive. The woman called authorities when she found the man after hearing scratching under her home.

POLAND: What a pro! Real hot stuff. A Polish prostitute was hit with an $820,000 fine for unpaid taxes after years of being a "working girl." The woman told the tax office she has very "generous" clients. She even claimed that one customer paid her nearly $2 million over a five-year period. We never learned whether she paid the fine or took it out in trade.

ROMANIA: PHEW! We hope she is satisfied now. A 72-year-old widow watched over the body for two weeks of her deceased husband. She did this because she wanted to make sure he wasn't faking his death in order to start a new life with his mistress. The widow finally got the hint he was truly dead when the body started to decay. She then reported his death to authorities. Police ruled the husband had died of natural causes.

RUSSIA: This is a real May-December marriage. A 98-year-old woman who was very jealous beat her 78-year-old husband because he was allegedly eye-balling a lovely neighbor. In response the husband hit his elderly bride with a rolling pin. No report on whether an arrest was made.

SOUTH KOREA: OUCH!! It has been reported that woman allegedly cut off her husband's penis because he spent too much time playing golf. The woman who lives in the town of Yeosu, reportedly attacked the 50-year-old man with a kitchen knife as he slept and flushed the member down the toilet. Police say that the wife confessed to the crime with the excuse that her husband ignores her and left her broke.

SWEDEN: We wonder what her husband had done to her? A woman admitted stabbing her husband to death with a fillet knife she had received as a Christmas present from her employers. Swedish police said that after the attack on her husband, Jeanette Javell, 42, wrote a bizarre note to her boss stating, "Thank you for the Christmas gift...By the way it worked!"

SRI LANKA: Suspicious movements? A Sri Lankan man was arrested trying to smuggle more than two pounds of gold through airport security in his rectum. The 45-year-old was headed to India via the Bandaranaike International Airport, when he was caught with the gold up his rear end. Custom agents said they were tipped off by the man's "suspicious movements."

THAILAND: An ugly American if there ever was one? A U.S. tourist was arrested in Thailand's Phuket Airport in early January 2018, after he overdosed on Viagra, stripped naked and went on a rampage. It has been reported that Steve Cho allegedly shouted like a maniac and threw his own feces at airport security guards before he was arrested by police. PHEW!

TURKEY: Double Trouble? A convicted killer escaped from prison by switching places with his twin brother during a visit. The 19-year-old convict, Murat., had been serving time at a maximum-security prison when he and his brother apparently traded outfits. However, a guard later noticed that the twin's face looked slightly different. Both men are now behind bars, authorities said.

UNITED KINGDOM: A banana heist, maybe? In June 2019, a British man, Lawrence Vonderdell wrapped a banana in a plastic bag to simulate a gun in a stickup of a Barclays Bank in Bournemouth, official said. He bolted from the bank with $1,400, but later turned himself in. He was sentenced to 14 months for the totally bananas heist.

UNITED KINGDOM: They say this theft really hit home. It appears that the crooks in this heist did not just steal Widow Sonia McColl's belongings – they also loaded her 40-foot mobile home onto a truck and took off with that, too, said police in Cullompton, Devon. "I'm numb," said McColl, 70, who was not home at the time, "They've taken everything I've got."

UNITED KINGDOM: Idiot rightfully sacked for "Royal Chimp" joke. BBC Radio Danny Baker was fired in May 2019 in England after tweeting out a cartoon depicting the new royal baby as a chimp in a suit, with the caption: "Royal baby leaves the hospital." Archie Harrison Mountbatten-Windsor, born to Prince Harry and Meghan, Duchess of Sussex, is the first acknowledged mixed-race child in the royal family. Baker apologized explained that this was to be a joke about Royals vs circus animals in posh clothes but interpreted as about monkeys and race. Baker sounds like a racist.

ZIMBABWE: Guess they needed the dough? A gang of armed bandits robbed a bread truck and made off with 500 loaves. Lobel's Bakery was making a delivery at a shopping center near the country's capital city of Harare when several men hopped out of an unmarked vehicle, pulled pistols and took the loaves.

THE END

About the Author

Professor Birdsong received his J.D. from the Harvard Law School and his B.A. from Howard University. He teaches law in Orlando, Florida.

After graduation from law school he worked four years at the law firm of Baker Hostetler. He then entered into a varied and distinguished career in government service. He served as a diplomat with the U.S. State Department with various postings in Nigeria, Germany and the Bahamas.

Professor Birdsong later served as a federal prosecutor. After leaving government service, and before he began teaching, Professor Birdsong was in private law practice in Washington, D.C.

www.BirdsongLaw.com

lbirdsong22@gmail.com

Ordering Information

New books coming soon!

Dear Reader,

If you liked this book, I would greatly appreciate you writing me a review on Amazon or any other book site.

I look forward to sharing more funny stories with you in future books.

Thank you, I really appreciate your help.

Regards,

Professor Birdsong

Winghurst Publications
1969 S. Alafaya Trail / Suite 303
Orlando, FL 32828-8732
www.BirdsongLaw.com
lbirdsong22@gmail.com

Professor Birdsong's 157 Dumbest Thugs!

Books by Professor Birdsong

• Professor Birdsong's 77 Dumbest Criminals Stories (Kindle & Paperback)

• Professor Birdsong's 147 Dumbest Criminal Stories: Florida (Kindle)

• Professor Birdsong's 157 Dumbest Criminal Stories (Kindle & Paperback)

• Professor Birdsong's Weird Criminal Law Stories (Kindle)

• Professor Birdsong's "365" Weird Criminal Law Stories for Every Day of the Year (Kindle)

• Professor Birdsong's Weird Criminal Law Stories, Volume 2: Stories From Around the States and Abroad (Kindle)

• Professor Birdsong's Weird Criminal Law Stories, Volume 3: Stories From New York City and the East Coast. (Kindle)

• Professor Birdsong's Weird Criminal Law Stories - Volume 4: Stories from the Midwest (Kindle)

- Professor Birdsong's Weird Criminal Law Stories, Volume 5: Stories from Way Out West (Kindle)

- Professor Birdsong's Weird Criminal Law Stories - Volume 6: Women in Trouble (Kindle)

- Professor Birdsong's Weird Criminal Law - Volume 6: Women in Trouble! (Paperback)

- Professor Birdsong's LAW SCHOOL GUIDE: Techniques for Choosing and Applying to Law School

- Professor Birdsong's: IMMIGRATION: Obama must act now!

- Professor Birdsong's: 157 Dumbest Thieves!

- Professor Birdsong's: 157 Dumbest Thugs!

- Professor Birdsong's: 157 Dumbest Rogues!